BADLANDS

of the High Plains

Text and photography by Chuck Haney

FARCOUNTRY
PRESS

This page: Diane Gabriel Trail, Makoshika State Park, Montana.

Facing page: The Milk River flows easterly through Writing-On-Stone Provincial Park, Alberta.

Title page: Caprock hoodoo in Writing-On-Stone Provincial Park, Alberta.

Front cover: After a rainstorm, Painted Canyon in Theodore Roosevelt National Park, North Dakota.

Back cover: Cedar Pass, Badlands National Park.

ISBN : 1-56037-167-6
© 2001 FARCOUNTRY PRESS
© 2001 Text and photography by Chuck Haney
Book design by Lisa Mee

For more information on our books call or write Farcountry Press, P.O. Box 5630, Helena, Montana 59604, (406) 443-2842 or (800) 654-1105. Book catalog appears online at: www.montanamagazine.com

Printed in Hong Kong

Contents

Sunset on The Spires at Norbeck Pass, Badlands National Park.

Introduction

Badlands have always left powerful impressions on their viewers: good, bad, inspired, or just confounded. An amazed Captain Meriwether Lewis described the white cliffs on the Missouri River in future Montana as "seens of visionary inchantment" [sic]. The Lakota Sioux, while holding many important religious ceremonies at places like the Stronghold Table in South Dakota, also called the land "mako sica," or "land bad," which I presume meant scarce hunting. Indian fighter General Alfred Sully described the badlands in present-day North Dakota as "hell with the fires put out." Notorious western outlaws such as Kid Curry found the Missouri River's maze of concealed coulees a great location in which to hide from the law.

One constant in the badlands is change. In an arid land where erosion is king, come back to the same location next year and look closely. Things have changed. Wind and water constantly work at sandstone and clay formations to alter their sculpted bodies into new artistic forms. Erosion also unearths our planet's history. Stripped-down sedimentary layers reveal bones, fossils and an intriguing look back millions of years ago to when dinosaurs and a more temperate climate ruled these northern plains.

Some badlands don't give up their hidden secrets without a struggle. Their remarkable monuments and valleys are often located in some of the most remote regions of North America. Remote locations often mean primitive roads that can high-center a passenger car or bog down the mightiest of four-wheel-drive vehicles when wet. The infamous prairie gumbo can turn roadways into greased nightmares. Bentonite, a blue-gray layer of clay, makes up the slickest substance. This spongy clay actually absorbs sixteen times its own weight in water. This strange substance also hardens like cement as soon as the sun's rays dry it out. Gumbo is a microcosm of nature's forces at work in the badlands. Erosion and reformation.

Other badlands settings are much more accessible. Paved roads weave in and around remarkable country in national parks such as Badlands and Theodore Roosevelt, where herds of wildlife still thrive in spectacular settings.

From a distance, badlands can appear to be hauntingly harsh. Badlands demand a closer examination, where intricate details are revealed. From the diminutive Hell's Half Acre in Wyoming to the spacious Badlands National Park in South Dakota, each badlands area has a distinct feel and presence to it. To stand among towering pinnacles, pyramids and mounds in the badlands backcountry is to feel emotions and view scenes like no other. Intimidation, astonishment, inspiration and awe all at the same time. A simple twist of the heels gives a completely different look and feel.

Badlands to me are photographers' paradises and places that touch my spirit. An endless supply of angles from which to shoot the convoluted geometric forms produces new and exciting images. Fields of wildflowers complement the rugged countryside where dramatic storms add an intensity to both the actual shooting and the final image. First and last light of the day actually do make the rocks glow. Pure magic! Badlands beauty can be subtle like the call of a meadowlark on a calm morning, or stands of bright yellow prickly pear cactus blossoms. It can also practically hit you over the head with a shrilling coyote call, the petrified remains of giant sequoia stumps or the crack of thunder echoing across the plains. Yes, the badlands are like no other place. Enjoy the photographic journey.

Alberta

- *Drumheller*
- *Dinosaur Provincial Park, Brooks*
- *Writing-On-Stone Provincial Park, Milk River*

Many badlands areas are shaped by the rivers that run by them. The Red Deer River cuts a swath through central Alberta, exposing cliffs and badlands formations along the way. Starting from Island Buffalo Jump Provincial Park, the river courses southeast through the town of Drumheller. In Drumheller, the Royal Tyrell Museum of Palaeontology pays homage to the significant fossil and bone finds in the region, exhibiting nearly forty complete dinosaur skeletons. Just southeast of town are the small but spectacular Hoodoos formations. These pillars, called caprocks, are formed when softer rock erodes from beneath harder rock. They eventually resemble pedestals or mushrooms.

Around 13,000 years ago, as the glaciers retreated, water from melting ice carved the Red Deer Valley out of layers of mud and sand deposits. Today, the Red Deer River ambles past groves of stately cottonwood trees in Dinosaur Provincial Park. Dinosaur is the largest badlands area in Canada, and has been named a United Nations World Heritage Site. This popular park is one of the richest dinosaur bonebeds in the world and paleontology fieldwork reveals new finds and species on a regular basis. Hiking trails and guided tours lead through coulees and creek bottoms accented by an array of badland formations.

Near the Montana border, Writing-On-Stone Provincial Park holds a series of sandstone outcroppings along the Milk River, with the Sweetgrass Hills in Montana forming a pleasant scenic backdrop. Guided tours lead to an archaeological preserve where pictographs left by bands of Blackfeet Indians grace the sandstone walls. In fact, the more than fifty rock-art sites contain thousands of figures.

Dinosaur Provincial Park, refreshed by rain.

Evening sun highlights hoodoos of the Drumheller area.

Dinosaur Provincial Park.

Erosion is a constant force, as this storm-swollen creek in Dinosaur Provincial Park shows.

Drumheller hoodoos.

Welcome to the Alberta visitor center in Milk River!

Above and facing page: Dinosaur Provincial Park drama by night.

Facing page: Hoodoo south of Drumheller.

Day's end brings dramatic lighting to the Milk River in Writing-On-Stone Provincial Park.

Dinosaur Provincial Park.

Near Patricia, Alberta, in Dinosaur Provincial Park.

Above and below: Canoeing is a way to explore Writing-On-Stone, and Native American pictographs are one of the explorer's rewards.

A vista from Coulee Viewpoint Trail at Dinosaur Provincial Park.

Instant waterfall: gift from a thunderstorm at Dinosaur.

Dinosaur Provincial Park provides an abstract study for the lens.

Layers of long-ago ocean bottom at Writing-On-Stone.

A unique sandstone formation in the Milk River Valley.

Evening light near Drumheller.

Cap rocks in Dinosaur Provincial Park.

Red Deer River near Drumheller.

The Sweetgrass Hills contrast with Writing-On-Stone's sandstone layers.

Wind and water carved this Dinosaur Provincial Park sandstone.

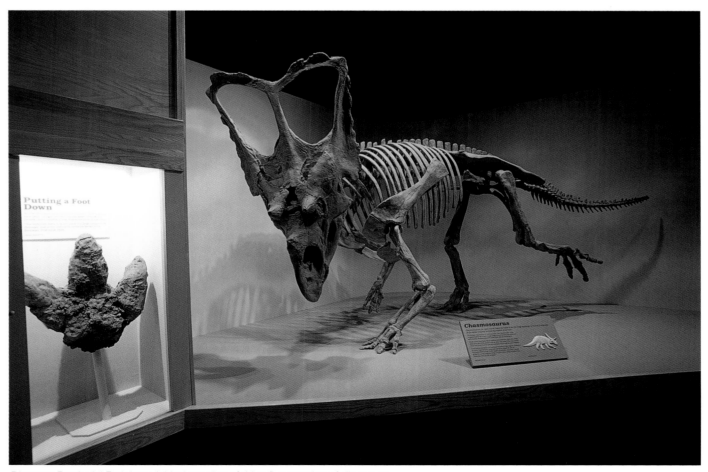

Dinosaur Provincial Park has yielded remains of thirty-five species of dinosaurs.

Skyborne beauties above the Milk River.

Hoodoos in Writing-On-Stone Provincial Park.

In Dinosaur Provincial Park, the warmth of sunset.

Above and facing page: Other-worldly shapes of Dinosaur Provincial Park.

Sandstone "monument" in Dinosaur Provincial Park.

Dinosaur Provincial Park.

Montana

- *Missouri River complex*
- *Makoshika State Park, Glendive*
- *Medicine Rocks State Park, Ekalaka*
- *Terry Badlands, Terry*
- *Jerusalem Rocks, Sweetgrass*

Montana's badlands are scattered among some of the most remote locations in North America. Travel to some of these locations, such as the Charles M. Russell National Wildlife Refuge and Missouri Breaks areas, requires a good map and luck with the weather. The legendary white cliffs of the Wild and Scenic Missouri River section require floating past in a canoe. The 149 miles of designated Wild and Scenic Missouri River, stretching from Fort Benton to Fort Peck Lake, contain long and narrow columns of dark rock called dikes that jut from hillsides, colossal buttes along the river's edge, and castle-like formations up in the coulees.

One of the most accessible badlands is Makoshika State Park located right outside of Glendive. Trails lead into such areas as Kinney Coulee, where artistic formations seem to change shape as viewers move around them. There are great examples of cap rocks throughout the park, and it also is rich in fossil and bone finds.

Medicine Rocks State Park is located north of Ekalaka on Highway 7. These amazing sandstone outcroppings resemble Swiss cheese, because the wind has carved them into strange and mysterious shapes. Legend maintains the Native Americans used the area for vision quests and considered the rocks to be sacred. Sioux warriors reportedly camped here seeking guidance from their medicine men before the Battle of the Little Bighorn.

Terry Badlands is located on Bureau of Land Management acreage just north of the town of Terry. A rough road leads to outstanding views of badlands and the Yellowstone River below. This area can look vibrant when ample spring rains green the grasses, and the yellow flowers of prickly pear cactus bloom.

Just east of Glacier National Park, on the Canadian border, the little-known Jerusalem Rocks cluster on the Canadian border outside the town of Sweetgrass. These eroded sandstone outcroppings line the north side of a coulee, with the Sweetgrass Hills forming a nice backdrop to their east.

Rising sun lights the Wild and Scenic Missouri River.

A sandstone spire in stormy light along the Wild and Scenic Missouri River.

Sandstone layers on a cold day in Buckley Coulee of the Jerusalem Rocks.

In the Terry Badlands, prickly pear cactus protects its bright blooms with spines that easily pierce moccasins.

Easter Island shapes in the Jerusalem Rocks.

A kayaker in the Wild and Scenic Missouri River.

Above: Cottonwood trees mark the Wild and Scenic Missouri's course.

Facing page: Terry Badlands dressed for spring.

Neats Coulee in Chouteau County near the Missouri River squeezes a hiking party into single file.

A thrilling light show over Makoshika State Park.

Makoshika State Park.

Yucca in bloom means it's summertime in Makoshika State Park.

Above: Female pronghorns (often called antelope), at home in badlands and on prairies.

Left: A storm drags an eerie shadow across the banks of the Wild and Scenic Missouri River.

Brightly lighted cap rock rises above Hell Creek State Park on the Missouri River.

LaBarge Rock above the Missouri was named for Captain Joseph LaBarge, whose steamboats passed this way for half the 19th century.

Above: Sage grouse hen waits at a lek, the dancing ground where males will court her.

Left: Diane Gabriel Trail, Makoshika State Park, honors the memory of the young paleontologist who excavated the Triceratops fossil now exhibited in the park's visitor center.

Above: Prickly pear cactus.

Right: Sculpted by erosion in Kinney Coulee at Makoshika State Park.

Above: "Bowling ball" rocks on white sandstone at the Missouri River.

Left: Hole in the Wall, above the Wild and Scenic Missouri River.

Evening light inflames Dark Butte along the Wild and Scenic Missouri River.

In the Terry Badlands, red cliffs greet the morning sun.

Medicine Rocks State Park near Ekalaka is named with the translation of a Native American term for the area.

Prairie sunflowers on the Charles M. Russell National Wildlife Refuge by the Missouri River.

The Missouri Breaks once provided hideouts for cattle rustlers and other ne'er-do-wells.

On the Oglala National Grasslands near Crawford, clay and sandstone formations intermingle.

Nebraska

- *Chimney Rock National Historic Site, Bayard*
- *Scotts Bluff National Monument, Scottsbluff*
- *Toadstool Geological Park in Oglala National Grasslands, Crawford*
- *Hudson–Meng Bison Bonebed, Crawford*
- *Fort Robinson State Park, Crawford*

*L*ocated in the panhandle region of western Nebraska is a remarkable country of spires, monuments and vast prairie that traditionally marks the end of the Midwest and the beginning of the West. Sandstone monoliths such as Scottsbluff and Chimney Rock were beacons for wagon trains traveling west along the Oregon Trail in the 1800s and are now American icons. At over 95,000 acres, the vast Oglala National Grassland in the northwest corner of the state is home to a variety of badlands. North of Crawford, Toadstool Geological Park is nestled up against the Pine Ridge. Dry creek beds wind past twisted rock formations formed by ancient volcanic flows that create an almost lunar landscape.

At the Hudson–Meng Bison Bonebed over 600 bison died in a small arroyo. The site was first thought to be a bison jump used by Native Americans, but scientists now concur that a prairie fire or lightning strike caused this bison herd to perish almost 10,000 years ago. An enclosure has been constructed to protect excavation of and research on this mass of bones. The drive to the site is lovely, through a stunning section with rock formations on both sides of the road.

Fort Robinson State Park was the site of the murders of famed Lakota warrior Crazy Horse in 1877, and of Northern Cheyenne men, women and children in 1878. The fort has been meticulously restored and is now one of Nebraska's most visited parks. The White River flows past the majestic Red Cloud Buttes, where fields of wildflowers accent the beauty of the scenic Pine Ridge.

The rugged forms of Toadstool Geological Park in Oglala National Grasslands.

Below Red Cloud Buttes in Fort Robinson State Park, hoary vervain blooms.

Cloudy day's end at Oglala National Grasslands.

Layers upon layers in Toadstool Geological Park.

The ongoing dig at Hudson-Meng Bison Bonebed, near Crawford, where more than 600 bison died 10,000 years ago.

Toadstool Geological Park's land often is called a "moonscape."

Scotts Bluff National Monument, near Scottsbluff, is named for an early–19th-century trapper, Hiram Scott.

Looking across the North Platte River from Bayard.

Chimney Rock, near Bayard, was the landmark telling wagon-train emigrants they were leaving the relative ease of prairie travel.

The badlands of Oglala National Grasslands are both beautiful and foreboding.

North Dakota

- *Theodore Roosevelt National Park*
- *Little Missouri National Grassland*

Theodore Roosevelt National Park is named for our 26th president, who spent a few years hunting and running a fledgling ranch in western North Dakota during his young adulthood. Acknowledging that the rugged badlands had quite an influence on his life, Roosevelt once said, "I never would have been President if it had not been for my experiences in North Dakota."

The park consists of two units. The South Unit is located an exit ramp away from Interstate 94 at the charming village of Medora. A loop drive leads past a land churning with life, where visitors view herds of buffalo, towns of prairie dogs and a whole host of prairie fauna. The Little Missouri River cuts a swath past the sculpted Wind Canyon, and panoramic vistas include a variety of badlands. Bright red mounds of scoria that accent the hillsides formed when seams of coal were struck by lightning and burned underground, sometimes for many years. Hiking trails lead into the heart of the country where wildflowers and cactus blossoms rise alongside shards of petrified wood. In the wilderness section of the park, look for the petrified forest of ancient sequoia stumps.

The park's North Unit is located near Watford City. Here the Little Missouri River has cut deep gorges and canyons that add to an already dramatic landscape. Round rocks called cannonball concretions weather out from huge slabs of sandstone. Like the South Unit, this area teems with wildlife.

Tying the units of the national park together is the Maah Daah Hey Trail that traverses the backcountry of the Little Missouri National Grassland. Travel by foot, mountain bike or horseback into a remote country filled with secluded valleys that brim with wildflowers in early summer. Fantastic badland formations seem to pop out of the prairie landscape all along the route.

A double treat at Theodore Roosevelt National Park, South Unit.

Above: Theodore Roosevelt National Park, South Unit, settles in for night under a pastel sky.

Facing page: Little Missouri National Grassland in western North Dakota protects 1.2 million acres of badlands such as these, along with prairie.

Above: Viewed from Wind Canyon Overlook, a fresh autumn snow touches the South Unit of Theodore Roosevelt National Park.

Facing page: One of Little Missouri National Grassland's spectacular sights.

A monument of nature's handiwork rises above the Little Missouri National Grassland.

Sturdy purple coneflowers are among wildflowers that thrive in North Dakota's badlands.

Above: Tough mountain bikes on the Maah Daah Hey Trail are one way to view the Little Missouri Grassland's China Wall formation.

Right: Seasonally muddy (like its bigger brother), the Little Missouri River traverses Theodore Roosevelt National Park, North Unit.

On the South Unit of Theodore Roosevelt National Park, a petrified tree,
and (below) a coyote—one of many wild creatures who live here.

A clear, brisk autumn day along the Little Missouri, Theodore Roosevelt National Park, South Unit.

Above: Spring blossoms brighten the South Unit, Theodore Roosevelt National Park.

Facing page: Cliff-top look across the Little Missouri River to Little Missouri National Grassland.

Above and right: Sunrise and sunset scenes in Theodore Roosevelt National Park.

Above: Black foxtail barley is a graceful ornament to North Dakota badlands.

Left: Is it possible for sandstone to glow from within? Theodore Roosevelt National Park, South Unit.

Above: Winter steals up on Theodore Roosevelt National Park, South Unit.

Facing page: Cannonball concretions, seen here in Theodore Roosevelt National Park,
North Unit, are cement-like rocks that built up around small organic items like leaves or shells.

Above: Fossilized leaves on sandstone near Lake Sakakawea.

Right: Red twilight adds to the eerie mood of Theodore Roosevelt National Park, South Unit.

Colossal natural construction above Little Missouri National Grassland.

Left: This bison calf, of Theodore Roosevelt National Park, North Unit, will someday stand about seven feet tall and ten feet long.

Below: Modern-day rough riders tackle Little Missouri National Grassland's Maah Daah Hey Trail.

Above: Frozen in sandstone are signs of waves ruffling ancient sea-bottom silt.
Theodore Roosevelt National Park, South Unit.

Below: Cow elk on the South Unit check out the photographer.

Facing Page: Chimney and cap rocks of Little Missouri National Grassland.

South Dakota

- *Badlands National Park, Cactus Flat or Wall*
- *Buffalo Gap National Grassland*

Perhaps the granddaddy of all the badlands areas on the northern plains resides just south of Interstate 90: Badlands National Park.

Almost a million people a year visit these very accessible and grand badlands. Dramatic landscapes are within windshield view as you drive Badlands Loop Road through this spectacular park.

A shallow sea, teeming with life, covered this region millions of years ago. When the creatures died they sank to the bottom and were covered in layers of sediment, becoming fossils. Eventually the sea retreated, exposing the one-time seabed. As the climate changed, the ecosystem evolved from subtropical forest to savanna, then to grasslands. Heavy rainstorms and winds now expose this land, revealing rich fossil soils that impart the colorful bandings that Badlands National Park is famous for.

This land is the heart of the Lakota people's homeland, and they continue to hold traditional ceremonies within this formidable landscape. Its peaks, gullies, buttes and grassy tables have evoked astonishment from people since humans began visiting the area. As conservation writer Freeman Tilden noted, it holds "peaks and valleys of delicately banded colors—colors that shift in the sunshine,...and a thousand tints that color charts do not show." Witnessing the sunrise or watching a full moon cast shadows across the architecture of these badlands can be a spiritual experience for non-Indians as well as for the Lakota.

Norbeck Pass, Badlands National Park, wears the cloak of sunset.

Yucca and pyramids of Badlands National Park.

Near Dillon Pass, Badlands National Park, hardy plants hang on.

Under Badlands National Park lie fossils of mammals that are 34 million years old.

Sage Creek Wilderness Area takes on autumn's tones.

Right: Who goes there? Near Dillon Pass, Badlands National Park.

Below: A rainy day isn't enough to stop this hiker near Sage Creek in Badlands National Park.

Buffalo Gap National Grassland lies to the east of Badlands National Park.

The Spires at Norbeck Pass, Badlands National Park—dramatic at sunrise.

Morning breaks over The Spires, Badlands National Park.

Near Cedar Pass, Badlands National Park, rock formations dwarf a hiker.

Nightfall silhouettes The Spires, Badlands National Park.

Wyoming

- *Hell's Half Acre, Powder River*
- *Vedauwoo Recreation Area, Medicine Bow National Forest, Laramie*

When you drive along Highway 20/26 west of Casper, Hell's Half Acre is easy to miss. A canyon literally hidden in the vast high plains, this badland is only 320 acres, but what it lacks in size is more than made up in content. Hell's Half Acre is one of the eeriest of all the badlands, causing its canyon to be chosen as a setting for several science fiction movies. Originally called the Devil's Kitchen for the fantastic color derived from coal deposits catching on fire, the site was renamed by President Warren Harding in 1923. Native Americans used the site as a buffalo trap, driving herds into the canyon from the sage-covered plains above. The area was a popular stage stop for early white settlers travelling between Casper and Thermopolis.

Between Laramie and Cheyenne lie the rocks of Vedauwoo, large jumbled piles of precariously perched granite boulders and artistic rock forms, some up to 500 feet high. The rocks are ancient mountains created from magma pushed up from under the earth, then weathered by ice, wind, and water. Scattered across the transition zone between the vast high prairie and the foothills of the Medicine Bow Mountains, these rocks were given the Arapaho word for "earth-born spirits." Native Americans believed playful spirits of man and animals created the formations.

Before they had the horse, Native Americans drove bison over cliffs into Hell's Half Acre to kill them for sustenance.

Left: Close enough to his den to pop back inside for safety, a prairie dog relaxes near Devils Tower.

Below: Rocky fingers reach for the sky at Hell's Half Acre.

Turtle Mountain and Vedauwoo Recreation Area in the Laramie Range.

Granite that is 1.43 billion years old makes up the towering rocks of Vedauwoo.

Hell's Half Acre could serve as the definition of rocky roads.

Sunset lights Vedauwoo formations on fire.